SELEC
POE

PENELOPE SHUTTLE

Selected Poems

1980–1996

Oxford   New York

OXFORD UNIVERSITY PRESS

1998

Oxford University Press, Great Clarendon Street, Oxford OX2 6DP

Oxford New York

Athens Auckland Bangkok Bogota Bombay Buenos Aires
Calcutta Cape Town Dar es Salaam Delhi Florence Hong Kong Istanbul
Karachi Kuala Lumpur Madras Madrid Melbourne Mexico City
Nairobi Paris Singapore Taipei Tokyo Toronto Warsaw

and associated companies in
Berlin Ibadan

Oxford is a trade mark of Oxford University Press

This selection first published in Oxford Poets
as an Oxford University Press paperback 1998

British Library Cataloguing in Publication Data

Data available

Library of Congress Cataloging in Publication Data
Shuttle, Penelope, 1947–
[Poems. Selections]
Selected poems. 1980–1996/Penelope Shuttle.
(Oxford poets)
I. Title. II. Series.
PR6069.H8A6 1998   821'.914—dc21   97–39071
ISBN 0-19-288076-4

1 3 5 7 9 10 8 6 4 2

Typeset by Rowland Phototypesetting Limited
Printed in Great Britain by
Athenæum Press Limited
Gateshead, Tyne and Wear

For Peter and Zoe

Contents

SELECTED
POEMS

Eavesdropper

Here is your face
wintering in a photograph,
alive and alone

I look at it,
at you as you were then,
and the midsummer opens,

pale feathers of ice fall
from the sky around me
and nearby, the ocean,

like a ghost's throat,
grows translucent.

Skeletals

Three skeletals are climbing
out of their blue and gold boxes.
They lift the lids of their coffins
and clamber out, naked,
each ribcage a cuirass of bone.
The central corpse
lifts up his arms in astonished blessing.
Behind him,
a tapestry of three-petalled flowers
flourishes,
trinity behind trinity.

3

And the celebration goes on,
the joyful pillage of golden light,
the rescue from a long deep dark,
the arrival into unfading colour
from the fastness of the sepulchre.

Three Lunulae, Truro Museum

Gold so thin,
only an old woman
would notice its weight

Crescent moons of gold
from the sunken district
of the dark,
out of the archaeologist's earth

The women of the lunulae
threw no barbaric shadows
yet a vivid dance
lit up their bones

I sense the mood
of many women
who wore the new moon
like a necklace

They have got over
the winter
while I still freeze

The slight quick tap
of a clock
goes on

like the rhythm
of an insect's leg
in the grass

I linger
in the locked room
of the gold,

trying to see,
beyond the sickle shapes,
the faces of three women

Sharp shadows breathe hard,
shedding skins like dusty snakes
Light twists in a violent retching

For an instant
there is the fragment of a lip,
an eyebrow fine as a spider's threat

A face like a frost fern

The custodian
locks the lunulae
in the safe once more

Cornish, they are,
he says,
dug up at St Juliot,
regalia of this soil,
and not for the British Museum

You buy me
a postcard of the lunulae
and we leave the museum,
enter the thin gold remains
of autumn

Rain

There is the thunder again
The rain falls
on the houses full of bags of bones
No one cuts flowers
The empty promises of the month
flush down beneath the streets,
through drains
The dots and dashes of the rain
are a waterlogged code

I am in the conscript army of summer
The rain dowses my fingerprints
Roses shudder, even the limbs of trees ache

On the shelf, the books are stern as cloud
I cannot read them

The rain stands miles apart from all the bibles
overcoming words with its own saturating argot

Appletree in America

An appletree by the roadside
and the road five hours travelling
out of New York City.

Here's a frontier,
this tree ripening
and the windfalls on the ground
like a first furnishing
in a continent
where I flit like a ghost
unanchored at twilight.

6

I hold a branch
and smell the apples,
watersweet, a beginning,
opening of energies
to rouse me from homesickness
as, beyond the roadside tree,
these foreign fields and hills
merge into the familiar loam of evening.

Honesty

What are these papery flowers,
thin stiff petals dry as insects,
these plants that rustle

as I pick them? Dry dilemmas,
arranged in a glass of water,
they go on puzzling me.

For days they are quite still,
unchanging.
They will not move in any breeze.

I see these nameless oval wafers
as if in an offing,
the most distant part of the sea
visible from the shore.

But when I touch their dry membranes,
they do not resist,
only fade and disintegrate,
finding the end of their pallor.

They are not unapproachable.
My mother says they are called 'honesty'.

7

Glass-Maker

It is no skill of mine,
glass-making.
I apprehend none of its craft,
transparency wiser than gardens.

To make glass
is clearer communication than speech.
A woman-maker of windows,
how would she look?

Angrily, piercingly at you
through her own upstairs window?
Or would she be smooth, hairless,
all bone, glabella?

Arduous manufacture, glass,
yet so simple to break.
Just strike it a glancing blow
and see the fragments, petal-less.

Are there glass-makers
on Arcturus or Aldebaran?
Does sun there sheer off unknown windows,
create blinding mirrors?

Dress me in glass!
Shoes, sleeves, all . . .
Let me move with great care,
interned in glass garments,
until I become glass.
my body made of glass,
cool and irreversible change,
glass eyebrow,
fingernail, clitoris . . .

Bone, blood and breath: all glass.
Until I am a devotee of glass,
reflecting all its famishings.

Downpour

A strong rain falls, a bony downpour.
The waters roar, like a riddance.
The day vanishes suddenly
and it is night that hesitates on a brink
for fear of difficulties. The rain, for instance.

Through the letter box, leaves instead of letters,
wet leaves blown along the path
and seeping through the low letter box,
an invasion that comes slowly,
but helped by the rain. The downpour.

I dream of thorns, aeroplanes and red horses,
but seldom of rain.
The creature spinning webs to catch its prey,
I dream of her also
but almost never of rain. The webs of rain.

The rain does not slacken. It has the scent
of mistletoe. But it is a weapon, thrown.
The windows shine black with it.
I sit watching the knotted bunches of rain.
I do not want to cease watching. Such brawny rain.

But the dry house, its music and its meals,
recalls me from the window,
draws me back from a downpour that is drowning me.
I prepare to turn from the window,
yet remain a moment longer,
looking at the blur of the candle-flame
against the dark glass.

There is the downpour. Here is the uprush of light.

November Poppies

I post my letters
and turn from the town,
from the wild children
in the schoolyard,
to the sea
and the first darkness
coming down on the water,
down from the harbour hill
unstoppable
like a young rider
clinging to the back
of his terrified horse.
The hills across the bay
are the colour of slate roofs,
blue and grey,
and watching them I hear
the winter earth echoing,
I hear it reading its sun and moon letters.
Again the twilight wind
menaces the water.
I open my mouth to taste its coldness
that leaves no poison on my tongue.

An hour later, I open my door.
I hope for a friend to join me,
to talk and joke.
But it is a stranger on the threshold,
an old woman with envious eyes
lifting towards me her reproachful tray,
offering me hundreds of poppies,
the reek of remembrance.

Four American Sketches

THE BLIND

The sun outstares me.
I pull down the blind.
Under these old afternoon clothes
my scarf-skin quivers.
My skin is thin and dry
like certain plants
and I fear the approach of my stronger self,
that reflection
who will flay me
until the flaps of my skin
bang like blinds
in a wind that doesn't care.

ONE OF THE NARRATIONS

These shrubs are unmarred by autumn.
A thousand narrations
might spring from their neighbourliness,
by my window.

But the shadow of my opponent
who wears my own inaccurate face
reaches out from unexpected hiding places,
ending my repose,
dragging me to sad locations
on the other side of the candle.

Here the autumn hobbles me.
All is cloudiness and the antagonist's hug.
We are face to face, she and I.
My dark side is towards the earth.

THAT NEW MOON

That new moon waiting for me
to step out into twilight
is no desolate island:

Not that little moon
around which the minnowy-blue sky flows,
no.

Nor is that new moon
made of snow.

That moon has the strength of a million spines.
It is this moon alone which stays awake all night.

NOVEMBER FIRST, NEW YORK STATE

Spurges, cascarilla, cassava:
the steepings of November,
mild disrobings, a damp natural air,
a day of reprieve.
A sour cold waits its turn
but today the mazes of autumn revolve.
Our personal effects are wedged into bright rooms,
the windows are wide open,
breathing the almost extinct summer.
You and I are reading the bibliotheca of autumn.

Cupboard Hyacinths

In the cupboard under the stairs
the winter flowers are crooning
in their cardboard pots.

In the fierce dark
the roots of the hyacinth are stretching
their green havoc.

I sit on the stairs
thinking of the garden beneath me
in the underworld of the cupboard.

I think how handsome
my hyacinths will be,
how they will tower over December
with a fragrance as heavy as Isis.

I will keep their corms from pestilence
because they contain my answers.
Without the bending Pisas of their stems
I will have too many questions.

I wait by the cupboard door,
I want to hear them grow,
I want to experience the cupboard's weather.

I want to carry my blossoming lamps
into the winter rooms,
their odour a guttural equilibrium
settling everything once and for all.

'The World has Passed' *

On the other side of the rose
there is the felling of trees

On the other side of the frost
there is the colour of a bruise

On the other side of the ovum
there is the woman of warfare

On the other side of the bonfire
there is the music springing back,
the retaliation

On the other side of the leaf
is the lesson in lacemaking

On the other side of the room
is a cabinet of curiosities, antique granary

On the other side of the mother
is a sigh full of filaments,
a few words walking on tiptoe

On the other side of the blackberry
is the harvest of the moon

On the other side of the voice
is the absence of the waterfall

On the other side of the ice
is the half-satisfied sea

* Yokut, American-Indian term for
'a year has gone by'.

14

On the other side of the blood
is the unrooted child

On the other side of the child
is the gulping-down of cloud,
the whispering of loopholes—
arrival at last at the fresh shrine

The Conceiving

for Zoe

Now
you are in the ark of my blood
in the river of my bones
in the woodland of my muscles
in the ligaments of my hair
in the wit of my hands
in the smear of my shadow
in the armada of my brain
under the stars of my skull
in the arms of my womb
Now you are here
you worker in the gold of flesh

Expectant Mother

In the stillness,
uterine,
hidden from me,
hidden from mirrors,
the foetal roots of wrist
and heart
are coiled within me.
They belong to the child,
to the incast,
a plumage of constellations.

I walk around the house
in bare feet
and a warm rope of blood
links me to my child

Rain falls on gardens and inscriptions
but I hold the edge of the rain.
I am a receptacle
in which other rain, amniotic, gathers,
for the one in his official residence
to enjoy.

I think of the quiet use of the unborn eyelids
and the stillness of my breasts that swell up,
a warm procedure of strength.

Already a name suggests its syllables,
but this remains secret,
a fishtail shadow,
a whisper between the night and the day.

First Foetal Movements of my Daughter, Summer 1976

Shadow of a fish
The water-echo
Inner florist dancing
Her fathomless ease
Her gauzy thumbs
Leapfrogger,
her olympics in the womb's stadium

The Orchard Upstairs

1

Here I meet no king-killer
Here I throw no shadow
Before birth, before the present tense,
I moved here amid darks, lunar dusk,
a ferret of blood, the unborn,
fenestella

2

Outside, the wind and the rain,
a darkness lurching against the threadbare house:
inside, the orchard upstairs

But I do not understand these fruits yet

3

Around the moon,
my dreams cluster, not moths
The antique photographs of the dreams
lead me always to this one room,
overlooking neglected lawn and pond

From a window I look down again
at the leafy air-raid shelter,
hear again steam trains shunting beyond the trees

Opening a door to a room in which apples are stored
in rows, I hear the stark cries of a woman giving birth

4
The room was cold, as if no glass
were fixed in the window frames
The room was damp, as if a fountain
sprang in the centre of the room
The room was draughty,
as if the house was fallen in ruins

I stand at the threshold,
lunar observer at the brink of apples

5
In the unused room
she laid out the windfall apples in rows
The silent house was filled with the scent of bruised apples
I climb the stairs
of a familiar house whose demolition approaches
My bones break with the bricks,
the foundations of my heart will crack

6
Something, a cloth, a veil?
chokes me
The doorways throb, like yew branches
in a storm
The old house eavesdrops
It bewails my thoughts

7

I do not sleep in this bedroom any more
But I shed skins here
I touch the skin of an apple
It is smooth as the ear of a hare

8

A woman in childbirth,
the difficult fame of labour
All night, all day, all night again:
the freshly-painted walls of the nursery
echo with her whorling cries

At dawn, a newborn howling amid
the apples of the future

9

The leaves scud before the wind
across the lawn,
leaves like birthmarks

10

A small speck or stain
on my heart,
it is my sadness for the lost room,
the pillaged house

What are the conditions for equilibrium?
Is there a balance among apples?

11

Like bone the stairs that I climb
and ice the banisters I grasp
Is it a garden of fruit trees I approach,
or is it a cemetery
   And the brightness of colour,
      is it life or death,
         that red?

12

In the morning, the sun cools itself
against the orchard mirror
I sit on the window ledge
and below me the lawn is calm green water,
a lake of old love

THE CHILD-STEALER (1983)

Twilight

The twilight
is like a fine rain
forcing us home.

Under the trees
glow the chalky threads
of snowdrops

at which I stare—
who goes there,
the sentry cries.

But how can I describe
the mastery of flowers
grazing the earth,

like translations done
without dictionaries?

Wings

On me
are beating the invisible wings
of the firstborn,
unique
as a distillate
of all the languages

and they are also
the heavy wings of stone
that pull me down
from my happy sojourn in the air
and drag me to the ground

I gasp and the hoop of breath
bowls me along

The Buds

In the ancient fuchsia bushes
there are always bees,
at any time of day.
The bushes are so old
they are turning into trees,
the stem of each bush
hardening into a gnarled trunk.
The pendulous scarlet-mauve blossoms
call the bees with their scents,
tuning-forks to the bee-songs.
My young daughter and her friend
pop the new buds in their firm fingers.
In response to my rebuke
they tell me, seriously,
that this helps the buds to grow.

Indoors and Outdoors

Listen, the snow-sheaves are rustling,
a frozen harvest.

And quietly, the snow is speaking.
Snow refuses to stand trial.

No matter,
indoors the furnaces are ready.

They roar in the basements,
enraged ancestors.

I listen to the sly ifs of fire.
I dance on hot coals,
skid over thin ice.

Indoors, the snow is afraid of me.
Outdoors, I fear the calamity of cold,
unignitable enemy.

Grosser ice encases the few twigs
of the thin bush by the back door.

The bird's abandoned nest
is thonged with ice.

Winter inherits the outdoors.
Indoors the fires are making themselves at home.

Märchen
or, The Earthborn

Our smart house new-painted chocolate brown
makes me think too closely of the Märchen,
of Hansel and Gretel, and the tasty roof;
of the maiden with no hands;
and all the dangerous defenceless ones
in those old and far-off tales.

Birds that were girls and boys,
bears and foxes that once were men;
girls who crouch in the kitchen ashes,
golden gowns hidden in nutshells,
these cruel and vengeful heroes and heroines.
In this half-light of a winter afternoon
I pity the old parents warily watching
their gleaming half-human young.

In an Old Garden

Lanhydrock House, Cornwall

A pewter urn
crammed with blue flowers
presided over
by two infant angels
brooding, chins sunk in cupped hands,
elbows propped
on the urn's discoloured rim.
Day after day they gaze
at these flowers,
sun baking their pewter wings,
rain dripping down
their cherub backs.
Buttocks perched
on sprays of iron leaves,
they freeze in winter,
but never lift their heads
from precarious contemplation.

No one disturbs their repose,
their steadfast response to the flowers.
The motionless sweetness of the twain
rules the garden like an enchantment.

Not born yet, my child,
my little dancer, equilibrist,

24

ever-mobile creature,
who will laugh at their solemn pose; dance,
and leave their spell unbroken,
the garden sustained by her guiltless glance.

Nude Study

Deep in it her skin
has that faint light left
when the sun has just gone
below the horizon.
She does not expect
not to be scrutinized.
For some she walks through the forest
following the tracks of the beloved,
touching wood all the time.
For others she is an echo of poverty.
Or she is simply statuesque, motionless
on her plinth,
maybe a dweller in heaven, maybe not.
She offers herself to some
like a scroll of ancient design;
to others as an old tax-demand envelope
covered with doodles.
For release she has only to speak.
This action will bring her freedom,
meagre, plain, bare liberty.
It is not indecorous to ask for this.
But neither is it dangerous to have her body displayed,
her silence unbroken,
her bones kept still for our enquiries,
the breasts casual, the knees braced.
Today her smile is uninflected,
neither listless nor deliberately appealing;
with arms upraised and pelvis tilted contemplatively,
she is utterly visible, perfectly eloquent.

Disembarkation

This white ship sails on a crimson sea.
There are no storms.

I crawl along the deck, peer in terror
over the polished taffrail.
This is no pleasure cruise.

There are no deckchairs in red and white striped canvas.
No traveller sips bouillon.
There is certainly no anchor.

A scarlet wake flares out behind us
and the ocean of red glows like grease.
My skin is like a statue of me.
Even if an ogre, the captain is invisible.

His ship's prow guts the ocean
as if each wave were a fish.
His ship crosses the seas, flat red lawns.
Always, this journey across leafless red,
the ship leap-frogging on.

Yet now it slows, sighs deep in its engines,
even this ship sighs, retchingly, and slows.
Stars, nebulae, appear in the sky.
And here are the lights of the land.

The ship loses its vigour
and all that strength comes to me!

Knowing nothing but strength, I jump for it.
Beneath my feet, the waves of clay dip,
almost throwing me to the ground.
I struggle to get my balance, gasp for air,
inhale the different bacillae of dry land.

(Out on the horizon, that ship,
the frigate of blood,
sails on over the humble water,
forever bound on its sluggish voyage.)

Preference

Preferring flowers,
I acknowledge meridians,
the continuous circles that cry
and come ashore amid blood.

Preferring flowers,
wild or cultivated,
I dab at weathers,
at careworn clouds.

Preferring flowers,
it is hard for me to fathom
the waves, their salt, their cunning,
the shores they determine and unfreeze.

Preferring flowers,
the sky unsettles me.

I prefer flowers
and the earth's monotony,
a life kept well within earshot of leaves.

But far out at sea
the future of flowers is planned,
themes of flowering
are rooted in the horizon.

I stand by the faggots of firewood
stacked in the yard by the door
but where in the world am I?

Am I beyond flowers,
here where the flames are born
in a shock of animal odours?

Must I acknowledge flame,
the molten, the furnace?
Recant those petals, blooms,
the softer fragrance?

Prayer

In the margin of the book
I sketch leaves, snowflakes.
This white page is a sleepiness
I want to awaken, but it is hard,
I dream only of wakefulness,
my inklings do not take hold.
Windows, mirrors, doors,
all openings like these distract me.
Hankering after order,
I remain haphazard,
charmed, enchanted by rumours.

Outside, the snow is not distracted.
It falls, intent on ending the thaw.
The grass disappears amid creases of snow.
It is, I suppose, disguised against its will . . .
And watching the winter settle,
I imagine myself in a rowing-boat,
the shore stretching back
into the sweetness of the past
as I embark across unfrozen waters.

I'm going somewhere unknown, untroubled,
mist rises from the kindly waters,
enfolds me in its secret placid linen.

The Gift

You don't want it?
It is too wayward?

Has too many double meanings?
Smells of a burning?

Rejection is your first thought,
no need for it, you say,
erase it, destroy it.

But be warned.
Its fragments will ache like utter distance.

These snakes are not harmless.
Those ladders lead somewhere.

Now the antiquities arrive,
with their cloudless apparatus.

Let them in oh let them in.

Ashes, Eggs

A phoenix the colour of blood
and the colour of leaves
rises again from the ashes.

Here are the wings.
Here is the new shadow.
Here are the bones.
Here is the new egg.

In some rooms, the egg
will grow to flesh and birth.
In others, to song alone.

In my room, I call up the creature.
Slipshod and wet, it may come to me
or go another way.
I can compel nothing.

Come, I say, come little life,
out of the ashes, out of the egg,
come and settle here,
you phoenix of women.

The Child-Stealer

Gossip, pure gossip,
words to be sewn on tight.

Behind the door,
a phlegm of yearning and terror.

A line of victims, waiting.

Out fall the babies.

Late at night, doors and windows
fly open to let her in,
Lilith, the child-stealer.

Gossip, only gossip.
Afraid of the ache?
It goes deep.

And who dares to be
where that ache lives,
is born among strangers?

Out fall the babies.
Out of the pattern.
Out of the circle.
Lost forever.

Out of the light.
Out of the mirrors.

Into the dark.
Lost forever.

They fall out of the women
on to the trembling pavement.

Why?
Blood rushes away with the answer.

Mother and Child

My heart sharpened to a point
and piercing you,
my child,
who came when I called,
in the moonlight, years past,
in the little bedroom,
in the whiteness of the full moon—
I knew your sex, your name:
the prophesying was easy.
Time has brought us onward,
in its own sweet and hard way.

And my anger pierces you,
and transfixed, you watch me,
on your guard—
I pull back my weapon,
my sharpened heart pierces itself
and frees you,
and you bound away,
singing one of your own wild unique songs.

The Children

In the boundless afternoon
the children are walking
with their gentle grammar on their lips.

From door to door
the little ones go, brightly tranquil,
repenting nothing.

How safe their journey,
their placid marching,
famous and simple voyage.

Whisper to me as if I were a child
and the answer you get
let it be your oracle and mine.

Panics may still trouble us,
the archaeology of our own past,
but we are pursuing that too-knowing adult dark
with the fires and lamps of innocence.

Soon our message will reach you, our gospel.
Free at last, happy at last,
we have gone away into the wise world of the children.

The Hell-Bender

It is an hour without heroes in an Ohio valley.

The hell-bender is there,
'a large aquatic salamander
about eighteen inches long and very tenacious of life'.

He is a summer beast
nimbly folding the water into shapes
that suit him,
his garments he might sleep or hunt in.
All feebler things are his serfs, his fodder.

(Your sigh glitters like sun on rapid glassy water,
in the valley the campers deliberate over maps;
the morning trembles in its hurt.)

The salamander pours himself through his waterfall prairies;
garden pools do not admit him
but anyway he, supple stone of blood, fiery rope,
streaks away from their logic,
away from the white proud superstitious flowers,
away from the hooded lips of the snapdragon.

He does not recognize his children
but shoots tumultuously through the water
as if his sister were with him.
He is the serpent of sun who lives in water,
he is a master of water and fire, cool heaven and hot hell;

He is clarified to his length, his spare eloquence.
He knows he will never die.
(Who said he is only a kind of fish?)
He darts through water like thread through a fine needle eye,
he is very tenacious of life.
He can bend hell.

Snake

Snake lazing in the wet grass,
less useful than cow or horse.

Line of silver on the family path,
silver as the Rio de la Plata.

Serpent silver as my ring, my bracelet,
laughing silently as those two circles.

Serpent tingling from place to place,
one of those who do not save lives,

at whom the countrywomen fling sharp stones,
but whose daughters greet with sudden smiles.

Creature more magic than mouse or rat,
more thoughtful than donkey or cat,

whose cry is mistaken for wind in the trees,
from whom so much has been stripped,

now you are only one limb,
one skein, one thumb,

you are a long thin silver skin,
a rod that works for god.

Because of your perfection
we say you possess venom and deceit

but whoever has perfection
can do without compassion.

Silver female with your nest of pure white eggs,
you live both by basking and gliding,

you die without screaming,
you come to an end,

your silver stiffening to pewter,
then thawing back into the shallows of earth.

Your young wriggle free,
bruised but seamless,
each one her own stepping stone.

The Vision of the Blessed Gabriele

Carlo Crivelli, National Gallery, London

In the evening sky, swallows

and the saint in his robes of evening cloth
gazing upward with his worried stare.

Is it because there is no star?

His feet have slipped out of their sturdy medieval scholl sandals.
He kneels on hard sand where thin grasses fountain
and starfishy cacti flourish near a few egg-shaped pebbles.

The frail tree that for years has borne no plums
touches both the saint's shoulder and the sky.
He is holding his hands palm to palm,

making the old holy arch of fingers and thumbs,
his two little fingers making an exact oval.

He looks up at her as if she's a trespasser,
hanging there in her larger oval in the sky,
the queen and her babe,
as if he sees her as the queen of untruthfulness.

How worried and angrily he stares at her,
his hands kept holy and invulnerable,
his bare feet ugly and ordinary, a man's feet
on a man's earth,
behind him the barren tree
and above him, she and her fertility.

Swags of fat fruit, unbelievable ripeness, loll across the sky
supported by an old ragged linen hammock;
hanging from the sky not stars but outsize heavenly fruit
knotted in a casual arrangement of dirty bandages.

On the sandy ground his holy book lies open,
forgotten, its script of red and black abandoned
as in horror he stares up at the fruit,
apples and pears from a giant's orchard.

Who put them there, apple and pear,
growing on the same branch, fruit bigger than a child's head?

The hedgehoggy halo of the saint quivers.

Within this glistening vagina the sky has blurted open
like an eye or a fruit, there is this queen or golden doll
carrying her stiff golden child,
golden and ruby-red couple in the sky,
cargo lugged along by cherubs, the crumpled robe
of the woman evidence of their haste.
They peer round the edges of the mandorla, singing a suitable song.

And like a gulliver the helmeted man
with his thoughtful grieving head
lies face down on the path in the wood,
alive or dead, who knows?

Not the saint, still staring up at the sky with its storm of fruit,
at the mother of gold, her foot set on fruit,
on another goddess's golden apple.
The child holds either a second golden apple or maybe a golden ball.

The saint gapes. This is the pain of the answered prayer.

In the pond by Gabriele's feet, in the green water,
the drake moves to the lustrous duck
with almost unnoticed longing, with vigilant love.

On the branch of the plum tree, a bird is about to fly away,
north to China or south to India.
When the bird has flown the saint will be able to weep.

The Weather House

for Peter

I usually understand you
when you are working with electricity
because we have often run away together
into the park of storms
where the thunder and his sister lightning live;
there the clouds come to us like pets,
eligible grey mammoths asking to be fed and groomed.
We build our weather house
from the shaking white boughs of electricity;
the branching sky alive with the sleepless storm
is our garden where we gather flowers of fire and hail.
When we fear our life is slipping
back into familiarity and calm ground

we return to the special house with its trembling galvanic rooms,
to the garden seared with the tallness of trees,
to ardent air prickly with hope of rain.
How the clouds crush us under huge pigeon-grey feet
before releasing their naked furnaces of rain on us,
till we are like fountains kissing!
How the storm aches with its own fame, its long steps
pouncing to reach us!
Electricity wires us, it shoots its fix into our veins
and our dreams lengthen into flooding weather, the sweet breath
of downpour, the waterfall gasp of it.
I usually understand you
when you are working with electricity
and despite the shocks
I clasp you in my arms, our skins jolting with the power,
sharing the voltage,
Storm the friend and lover of our hearts.

Selena

'her cherry's in sherry'—woman's period

The unripe cherry has the luxurious bitterness
of the earth's satellite, the scarlet morals of it,
its acid blotches stinging your tongue;
a moon cherry that mulishly leaves its flavour
in your mouth all month; and that secret early woman
in the sky, whose soft authority will not fly away
but who holds us in her strong birth-marked arms,
or hides us behind her natural naive skirts; that taste
of sharp cherries steeping our tongues only means
we are her namesakes, the selenas . . .

She is the poverty of an unimportant person,
a boy, say, or a simpleton, one grown but not
and never to be adult;
she may be persistent as a child that sucketh long,

or as reproachful as headmistress; her green-goose
ceilings and her books of grief are all her;
on these observatory nights when the taste of oboes
blots out what you said or might have said to me,
she falls in scalding rain, she approaches the waning sea,
accepting without protest her unprotected position.

She stands before us, a sudden window, an intense door;
though she lets nothing ever be quite closed or quite open.
There is always one more letter to be learned
in her alphabet, one next fruit to be tasted;
after the sour text of the cherry, the golden and tiring orange,
the juicy pang of the scarce pear, the pearly apple's
pedestrian-calm;
the clingstone peach with pink and velvety skin;
her hands offer a midnight feast, her bride's charm.
She is almost capsizing with the fruit she brings.

All her roamings lead her to richness,
a richness that, as soon as it's at its height,
begins to diminish, little by little, until it becomes
another currency, another night's work in a sky so intimate
it reaches the most sensitive part of the world, a leaf maybe,
or a fish sleepless in his ocean,
or a pillow-slip blowing in the wind that has waited an eternity
    on the line
for this touch of moonlight on the worn white tucks and embossings
    of its linen,
selena's touch, her concubine's breath,
her fruits and their felicity.

Disdainful Jack

After the painting, Our Jack, *by Henry Scott Tuke,*
depicting Falmouth-born Jack Rolling on the quay punt Lily,
off Custom House Quay, 1886

The boy in the bright blue coat,
navy-blue cap jammed on cropped head,
right hand hooked loosely in the rigging,
boy with his sad monastic look,
his uncomplaining expectant stare,
his knowledge of blue.

Behind him, over his shoulder,
rises the terraced harbour town,
its royalist church and roughcast houses.
Its unsheltering streets
only numb or vex him.
He has no time for the land, nor it for him.
Ashore, he trips facetious in clogs,
but on deck his feet are light and undisabled.

With little humour and less hope,
he stares disdainfully at the painter, at us.
He dwells on the voyages he's chosen,
the hammock he'll be suspended in,
the little whips of salt already burning his lungs.

He has no time for luck.
His look tells us that, plainly.
He watches the waves,
his eye forming its own past tense,
looking beyond Tuke
far out to sea,
to the day or night of his drowning.

In blue jacket and blue hat,
dressed for sea and sky,
Jack's at a standstill, lounging stiffly,
prisoner of his own dignity.

He has no sweetheart.
He keeps his energy for knowing the sea.
His gaze is the narrow ledge along which he inches his way,
lonely but used to it, to the narrowness,
the fear of missing his step.

How the ocean will welcome Jack,
who knows the cues of the drama,
who appreciates the cabaret of storm,
the syncopation of the tides.

Only when the waves close over his head
will he smile, relax, at last open his heart,
find his expected home, his unexpected happiness.

Wise sailor, he never learned to swim
and so can sink without a struggle,
the fraternal waves letting him down gently
on the rope of his last breaths,
Jack safe forever now
in one of the galleries of the sea.

Horse of the Month

Here is a horse made of sleeplessness.
He is devoted to me.
I am sewn to his saddle,
am his established rider.

Breathing upon the sky,
the horse makes me love him.
He repeats his breath of flame.
The sky is burning, old shawl.

The trash and dust of smoke
is luck on our tongues.
The horse begins to speak, composedly.
We ride down green lanes, clover byways.

I ride him like jewels.
We wheel around our red-coral valley,
inseparable, sleepless,
grass turning to fire wherever our hooves of blood fall.

Orion

Orion standing at ease
just above the horizon.

Offer the dreamer
a window
through which she may see
the most secret parts
of the warrior.

Orion,
the within-er,
the penetrator.

The god's cool semen
falls upon her,
he throws it upon her
as if flinging
the last drops of wine from his cup.

Her dream will come true.
A child is waiting for its life.

The thunder-lord of stars is wailing,
changeling caught by flesh again.

Giving Birth

Delivering this gift
requires blood,
a remote room,
the presence of overseers.

They tug a child
out of the ruins of your flesh.

Birth is not given.
It is what is taken from you;
not a gift you give
but a tax levied on you.

Not a gift but a bout
that ages both the contestants.

Birthshocks hold on tight, for years,
like hooked bristles of goosegrass,
cleavers clinging to your skirt and sleeves.

The raw mime of labour
is never healed,
in giving birth
the woman's innocence goes,
loss you can't brush away,
it stains all your new clothes.

No longer can you be half-woman, half-bird.
Now you are all woman,
you are all given away,
your child has the wings,
can resist the pull of the earth.

You watch her rush up,
clowning her way through the cloud.

And you applaud.

Chrysalis

Like all mothers
I gave birth to a beautiful child.
Like all mothers
I wiped myself out,
vanished from the scene
to be replaced by a calm practical robot,
who took my face,
used my bones and blood
as the framework
over which to secure
her carapace of steel, silicon and plastic.
I was locked out of her clean carpentry
and smoothly-reprimanding metal.

Yet that robot's rude heart
flowed with love's essential fuel
because my child was one of the millions
of beautiful children
and knew how to tackle the machine.
She embraced the robot woman lovingly
each day
until her circuits and plastics wore away.
Now the soft real skin can grow,
the blood and breath move again,
the android is banished.

I emerge from the chrysalis
and go forward with my child
into the warm waters of the sea
in which we are both born at last,
laughing, undamaged,
bathing alive in this salty blue,
my motherhood born out of her,
her woman's name and noon out of me.

Child and Toy Bear

It is essential
to have the bear
in the bed
though he is nameless
and disregarded throughout the day.
At night he must lie beside her
so that she can sleep,
his black nose firmly clenched
in her hand,
the spar that keeps her afloat all night.

Miss Butterfly, Miss Moth

Butterfly and moth,
one primrose pale,
the second grey as god himself,
both dead,
the child keeps them
in a Flora carton
with air-holes pierced in it;
airy tomb,
plastic sepulchre
she has given to moth and butterfly
as a sanctuary
where they can find peace,
transform to their next stage
which, she sings hopefully,
(Miss Butterfly, Miss Moth),
will be fairy or elf
but fears will be only wing-tip dust,
a tick of mist;

for the child has undreamed her song before.

Bear-Hug

Childlessness crushed me,
a bear-hug

I never breathed
till I bore her

though now in her clasp
I hurt

being drawn so far
from my breathless life

Why compose
on a guitar
at six years old
a curious refrain
entitled
Horse Mane?

But she does

The Child

1

Elaborate manifestation of a smiling dog
clockworking his way over the carpet;
he crouches and barks in a high peeping metallic woof;
the child follows the toy into the room,
remarking calmly, he's really a hedgehog, you know . . .

2

The wind windowed me out
but I held on to my friend
or my friend held me with his teeth.

Did it hurt, I ask.
No, she says, it didn't.
Landing safe in the net of her dream.

3
Or she dreams of the cat,
his dovetail pleasures.

She dreams I was angry with her.

She dreams she had an egg
which hatched out into a nasty chick.

She dreams she was given another egg.
And all the other children had eggs too.

4
Another dream (she said)
was when I had a little cat
that got smaller and smaller
and ran into the bush;
when I called it
lots and lots of little dogs came out.
Sober dream dogs,
gentle canine companions.
In the child's dream they bark quietly.

5
As soon as she wakes
she starts up all her unmarried nonsense.
The rebellious parents
have to find all she needs,
her props;
they puff up and down stairs,
supplying dolls, pearls, frogs, rice, birds.

To the child nothing is a luxury,
every thing is a necessity.
For her, each day has the glamour of convalescence,
all conversations possess the repartee of scripture.

Masks

The child has masks.
It is easy to forget this.
Behind her masks
of today and tomorrow
is yesterday's face,
see, she is still too young
to understand anything
but food and sleep.
My threats are no way
to break her silences,
to curb her fires,
there must be a way
of speaking
that runs true and clear
from the womb's infant
to the child who faces the world,
her school masks of fear and pride
sprouting fresh each day;
she flinches but does not retreat;
she wears a bruised lazy-mask,
a stiff oldfashioned anger-mask,
one summer mask glitters, gifted with speech,
another is a poke-tongue laughter mask.
She has her heroic silver bedtime mask.
My own pedantic mother-mask watches.

There must be a language
for me to speak, for her to utter;
a language where the sweet and the bitter
meet; and our masks melt,
our faces peep out unhurt, quaint and partial as babies.

Act of Love

At night, riding our bed like a willing and dethroned horse,
we are secret depositors proud of our flaws,
flaws that scratch a diamond;
you are a stinging mirror to me, I another to you.
We are each a bird ruthless as cat
but we let that cruelty go into the dark
and lie lithe as lizards, side by side,
our fingernails extracting silver from our hearts,
the distinctive lode we work,
darkness arcing with our buck and doe brights
until we rest for a little, partners slumped on the ropes of
   night's ring.

Our outstretched arms anchor us, inseparable;
my nipple is hard as diamond, treble and desirous;
my breast-skin soft as unchaperoned moss;
your hand on it a serious shimmer;
my breast grows newer, newer,
my yanked-open laceless nightgown's bodice,
its cotton seam is caught tight around my ribs
where my heart is beating gravely and loudly,
its blood full of steadfast strength and mystery.

The night outside is a teetotal drum we flood into silence
as your delicate hard sex presses against my hip;
when we meet and join we hold our breath,
then breathe out all the burning novelty of our bodies,
a big vapour furling into the room, flag
made from our clear-sky flesh, our unearthly diplomacy,
our hauntingly-real fuck;
I watch my familiar but elaborately-lifted leg
misty and incredulous in the straight-faced dark.

And as we are not blind or dumb
this is the time we stare and cry out best
as we wear out our weariness with thrusting,
our eyes open and glossy, our throats humble with aahs,

sighing into inaudibility, our lips soft reams
of silence; we're giddy with our tongues' work,
as if two serpents had become brother and sister . . .

As we cast ourselves into the night and the act,
our smooth knuckles shine,
we are gasping as we smell the sleep to come,
waiting for us beyond this untraceable room;
now we clamber the summit of old-friend mountain,
rising faster in our clamour,
swinging locked-together in our bell-apple nakedness,
in the double-pink hammock of the night
made of touch and breath,
(the purposes of the engineering!),
a labour of love as we rush towards that trembling edge,
toppling over yelling into the fall, the rapids,
the waters we enter, fluid as them,
my sex hot and hidden, perfect and full,
the corner of our sinews turned,
a clear answer found, its affirmative leaping from our mouths,
my body's soft freight shaking and accepting
in the clairvoyance of orgasm,
and your answering sheer plunge from mountaintop
into river,
flowing where the bed was.

Sleep takes us then and drops us into its diocese,
drops us from night's peak into a dawn
of martial ardour, of trees mad
with old-clothes spite, a morning
where the starving still wait for us,
each with their lonely cloudy gaze.

So only the sugars of the night offer us any breakfast,
only our night's act of love feeds us,
the remembrance of our bodies like slow-moving turtles
lifted from the sweetness of a sea of honey,
flying into more sweetness.

Only the touchwood of our sweet bed
dams the savage sour torrent of the day.

In the morning we must say goodbye, not hello,
goodbye until the untouchable day has gone
and the night recalls us again to our study,
to our sweating gypsy-wagon sheets,
our navaho pillows and rich pastures,
the mintage of our wild skins.

The Martyrdom of St Polycarp

He had known John
and others who had known the Lord
but he was betrayed by a servant,

arrested late in the evening
at a farm outside Smyrna,
hens scattering in panic,
geese retreating angrily,
children peeping from corners
to find out who are heroes,
who are villains.

This happens around the year 155,
the arrest of an old man
who had known those who had known
the Lord,
had known John.

In the city
a crowd assembles for the games,
officials, wives, magnates, courtesans,
labourers, idlers, children, artisans;
animals baying, trumpeting,
the stench not a clean farmyard stench

but a festering stink,
the reek of a blood circus.

The old man and the proconsul converse,
they see eye to eye,
they are the only philosophers
within five hundred miles,
and able to bear their differences,
the roman reluctant
to condemn the venerable man
whose honour he can see.

The old man shrugs, smiles.

'How can I curse Christ,
for in all my eighty-six years
I have never known him do me wrong . . .'

And the crowd is yelling,
                        'Kill him,
he is the one who destroys our gods . . .'

Even the cripples and lepers join in.

The circus gods need blood or ashes.

So because he is commanded
the proconsul orders the burning of Polycarp

'and the flames made a sort of arch,
like a ship's sail
filled with the wind,
and they were like a wall round the martyr's body;
and he looked, not like burning flesh,
but like bread in the oven
or gold and silver being refined in the furnace.'

He was like bread in the oven!
Like gold or silver in the furnace!

He turned the torture circus
to a fiery circus of joy, flames of the spirit.

But the cruel spectators did not clap their hands,
or fall to their knees, or say to the children,
look, there is a miracle, a man alive in the flames.

Did the people say, have our gods done such things?

Did they warm themselves at those flames?

The old man stood
with the flames flowing round him
like a weir of fire,
sailing in his ship of fire,
safe in his tent of flames

as the outraged crowd damned him.

At a sign from the proconsul
(curious in private life
about the supernatural)
a bored boy-executioner
braves the miraculous ark of flame,
pierces the old man's heart,
freeing Polycarp,
who kicks his corpse aside
and becomes a soul
and the crowd go on cheering,
children laughing, the rubbish gods ungrieving.

Hide and Seek

The child might be hiding in the ship
or in the cave,
or in the garden where the morning-glory
will find him some pretty name;
he might be hiding in the tree
whose shed needles fall like quills
on to the pitch of the dry lawn;
he might hide in a tower
built by a father for a son who never appeared,
the son dreamed-of but never caught up
into the real photographs of life;
the boy might hide by the cat-happy door,
or find some waterfall behind which to shelter,
be shuttered-in by the sheer fall of water;
he must hide somewhere.
He is a virtual prisoner in the powerhouse of the page,
must hide from the words thumping and beating on his head,
but where shall he hide, this boy who has not yet learnt
how to talk like a child,
or discovered that an evasive answer is the best way
to get uninterrupted possession of your day?
He hides everywhere, primitive, prodigal,
playing any number of odd games
in the garden of the red-eyed fish, their pool of stone and weed,
or in the stables where three horses watch him,
startled but, like electricity at rest, intensely patient.
The child hides, underfed in his blue shirt and french trousers,
in the room where I expected to find anyone else but him,
even a flock of those glossy and black gregarious birds
or the stately golden sane old dog of our crazy neighbours;
butter-finger room I at once let slip away into dullness,
losing him, he is not even behind those rivals, the curtains.
The child hid in a ship
and sailed away over an ocean, beneath deep-sea stars,
into the tenderness of storms,

the tempests, the burning calms,
the retentive and temperamental weather of a child
for whom no reward was offered and to whom nothing was promised.

The Lion from Rio

Golden inclination
of the huge maned head
as he rests against my knee,
his massiveness like feathers against me
amid this Rio crowd
through which he came to me,
this lion, my lion,
my lion of lifelong light,
padding unnoticed through the carnival.
Now his beast head rests in my lap,
golden flood, I am laden with it.
Looking up at me with his gentle puzzled gaze,
he says helplessly, but I am a man, a man!

My own child could have told me.
He was a man.
How could I not have seen it?
Listen again, he is drowsily moaning,
I am a man.

August Boy

The forest of summer is its own weight in gold
and you have climbed the tallest tree at noon
to bask above me and to kiss heaven, the fiery alpine.
High spirits! Silent golden child,
odd smiling pondering boy blossoming in a tree,
what country have you left to come and dwell here

in the burning branches and lion breath of the woods?
Child, boy, son I shall not carry, bear or nourish,
glowing ghost, summer boy who beckons to me
as I stand watching, soles of my feet scorching on the sandy path,
I know you are not a child I can claim,
you are not a child of the flesh, the fierceness of that.
Child without questions, child vigilant in a tree,
amazing as any thing made of gold, you live where the future is,
with all its carelessness and charm, its mistrust of direct answers.
The summer will not leave you behind, you are where summer is,
you are the heart of its heart, riding your solar beast,
the thoroughbred summer.
When I ask you your name you smile and say, 'you know my name'.
Furnace-Page of the Green and Gold of August,
Seigneur of the Summer, young Caesar of the Blazing Leaves,
wild, lenient and motherless, I recognize your boyish title.
Eagerly, easily, I lose my heart to you, my Heatwave Cupid.

Jungian Cows

In Switzerland, the people call their cows
Venus, Eve, Salome, or Fraulein Alberta,
beautiful names
to yodel across the pastures at Bollingen.

If the woman is busy with child or book,
the farmer wears his wife's skirt
to milk the most sensitive cows.

When the electric milking-machine arrives,
the stalled cows rebel and sulk
for the woman's impatient skilful fingers
on their blowzy tough rosy udders,
will not give their milk;

so the man who works the machine
dons cotton skirt, all floral delicate flounces
to hide his denim overalls and big old muddy boots,
he fastens the cool soft folds carefully,
wraps his head in his sweetheart's sunday-best fringed scarf,
and walks smelling feminine and shy among the cows,

till the milk spurts, hot, slippery and steamy
into the churns,
Venus, Salome, Eve, and Fraulein Alberta,
lowing, half-asleep,
accepting the disguised man as an echo of the woman,
their breath smelling of green, of milk's sweet traditional climax.

Killiow Pigs

from Killiow Country Park, near Truro

Five adolescent suckling pigs
fanned out alongside their sleeping mamma;
each daughter big as an alsatian dog,
her five petticoat-pink starch-skinned girls.
They sleep with resolution and vitality.
Our admiration does not wake them.
Fed on apples, their flesh is ready-seasoned.
This afternoon heap of pig breathes a clean dusk
into the air; spring and dung,
rhododendrons, sour vapour of swill and straw.
With their sexy squiggle tails,
their ears soft as cats but big and lopped-over
like ambitious rabbits, with their long carefree
strokeable backs, their feet comic and smooth,
snouts succulent,
these sisters lie outspread, five cordial orchids
against mother's blushing pungent bulk,
dreaming of orchards
where an exiled male roots and roams,
his boar thighs tough and angelic,
his head lowered to the cool brisk echoes of morning,
his ringed nose a gleam of gravity,
his sudden stillness all swinish magnetism.
Dossing mother and daughters quiver in sleep,
the juice of desire lolloping over their lips;
snouts swell with love; tails uncurl, grow fine
and tender as silk;
each meets her orchard lover,
dreamy pigs in their matrilineal slumber.

As we watch these females, hope and desire
rise in us, a cloud of matrimonial heat,
blossoming and getting the better of us,
oh these shameless porcine arrangers of marriages!

Alice

I live in one room.
My bedroom is my kitchen,
my study is my bathroom.
I am absorbed by my own powers,
feeling beautiful and resourceful.
I am awaiting an avalanche of young.
In me fifteen new hearts beat.
My stretched belly-skin is near splitting,
my bulk is pastoral, I know.
I smell of melons and cheese.
I am not restless or nervous.
I look pityingly at you
who don't possess my one room.
Soon there will be such a squall of piglet,
a shoal of tails and tingling ears,
an april fall of flesh,
a sixty-legged blind creature,
not a scratch on it;
a chute of pig, shriller than puppies,
fitter than fleas. I know all this
from previous experience.
Every one of my imminent litter will possess
our breed's gift for caricature.
The dog will turn and run from their chaos.
They will not be dangerous in their cherry-pale
and sugar-bright skins; but loud.
In the paddock they will race and scamper.
Like mine, their lives will be immensely public.
Under the afternoon sky they will sleep
as babyishly as in any cartoon
that would bonnet and bib them,
as if their flesh were lifelong safe, inedible,
and myself, Alice, their mother,
a human mother resting with full breasts bared
and aching in the flickering shade of the mimosa tree.

Alice's Husband

He is both predictable and unpredictable.
Both gracious and fierce, heroic
and brutal, a gothic husband.
Just when I have forgotten him, he returns,
savage and hopeful, pale both with lust
and with an aesthete's melancholy. This
was not necessarily his idea, he means. Elvish,
his turn of head; his glance by turns
high-souled, gloomy, flirtatious, deferential.
Glowering, he sniffs towards me. Ringed,
his snout is merely embellished, not owned.
He draws my smell into his nostrils
with a shudder of scandalized disbelief,
then trots a little closer; all this
surveillance! He moves forward, he who
has no after-life. His back is long,
his thighs huggable, his tail a perfect solo,
his odour of honey, pepper, camomile and wax,
a reek of desire, my infinite temptation, his bait,
this fallen angel of the pigs.
His testes are charming, burly,
they billow out, ballooning
from sudden excess of emotion; his plum-coloured
tongue lolls.
His powerful torso is like the beginning of flesh,
his massive capable jaws good as any dog's;
distract him from me now
and he'll charge you, speed and force, for the kill.
He is the axe at my root. His weight on me
is aficionado, apostle, family-man,
a giant refreshed.

God Dividing Light from Darkness

Michelangelo

An old man,
a feeble agèd grumpy
grimacing old god in the clouds,
cloud-bearded, lear-haired,
clambering through womb-mist,
fumbling, lost, tunnelling
through epiphanic coils,
their foams and jades and grimes,
their hulled and frilled scapes.

As old as these nesting clouds
that water-lily the void together,
he throws up his fog-robed arm
and delivers the world;
out of the womb-age of the old god
comes a cloud of earth and sea,
sky and dream,
ripple of sand and ripeness of rock,
fissure, passage and cave,
leaf and coriander seed,
swamp and hedgehog, etcetera . . .

He bears this child of his old age
without tenderness,
enraged, his heart closing
like a book of stone,
his eyes changing colour each instant,
flickering kaleidoscopic lightning;
his robes radiant waves
of cold-rainbows,
this frowning merciless old father,
minus cherubim,
bristling with opposites, the pangs of creation,
the light his perfect son,
the dark already too bad to be named,
serpent turning and grinning,
prodigal on the balance-scale.

Snakes and Quakes

Anything that wriggles
might be a snake.

Our yard grass whispers
serpentine, stern; seeding
into neighbours' neat gardens.

Coil of cloud returning
with rattling-tail;

the rain a green viper
withdrawing from life,
reclusive in the water table.

Around the new moon,
a snake of light
shakes and

the air cracks its whip;
window glass shatters;
buildings shake and boom.

The snake opens his eye.

Houses, ready to fall,
exhale the scent of him,
that breath of earth.

I sip water,
fearing everything but the snake.

I hold him,
spin in woman circles with him;
his hard dry lip against mine,
his tongue mustard,
colour and taste.

He sips my breath.

Doors move suddenly
with no help from hands;
the sky galloping,
rivers zigzagging,
the air's soft growl rippling.

Plumes of trees twist,
green and baffled.

But the serpent is already back
in his secret corner of thin air,
long-necked and unanswerable.

The earth locks its stable doors again.
The horse of quake gone.

I, snake-collared, yawning, garlanded
and sashed with serpents
invisible but coiling and scolloping
electric eelishness around me,
watch the golden worm of lightning (my beloved!)
fork his brazen tongue over the black sky,
lisping flame, stammering fire.

Thief

He will steal it, whatever you possess.
Whatever you value, what bears your name,
everything you call 'mine', he will steal.
Everything you have is frail and will be stolen from you.
Not just watch or bracelet, ring or coat,
bright objects, soft splendours, gifts, necessities,
but the joy that bends you easily and makes you feel safe,
your love of what you see each different morning

through your window, the ordinary seen as heavenly.
Your child's power, your lover's touch, will be stolen
from under your nose. He will steal everything.
He will take everything from you. You will never see him.
You will never hear him. You will never smell him.
But he will destroy you.
No surveillance is close enough, no guard clever enough,
no lock secure enough, no luck good enough;
the thief is there and gone before you have sense
of breath to cry out.
He has robbed you before, a hundred times.
You have never seen him but you know him.
You know his vermin smell without smelling him,
you know his smile of learning without seeing it,
you feel his shadow like deprival weather, grey, oppressive.
You know he watches from far away or from just round the corner
as you regather your little hoard of riches, your modest share
of the world, he watches as you build your shelter of life,
your hands raw from working day and night, a house
built out of bricks that must be guessed at, groped for,
loved, wept into being; and then upon those walls
you and your people raise a roof of joy and pain, and you live
in your house with all your ordinary treasures,
your pots and pans, your weaned child, your cat and caged bird,
your soft bestiary hours of love,
your books opening on fiery pages, your nights full
with dreams of a road leading to the red horses of Egypt,
of the forest like a perfumed pampered room wet with solitude.
You forget the thief. You forget his vanity,
his sips and spoonfuls of greed. But he watches you,
sly in the vaults of his wealth.
Shameless, sleepless, he watches you.
Grinning, he admires your sense of safety.
He loves all that you love.
Then, in disguise, with empty pockets, his fingers dirty
and bare, rings of white skin in place of gold bands,
he comes like a pauper on a dark patchwork morning
when summer is turning round and robs you blind.

He takes everything.
He is the thief in whose gossamer trap you have been floating
all these years. He comes and takes everything.
Your house is empty and means nothing, the roof falls in
and the walls of love dissolve, made of ice;
the windows no longer watch out over heaven, the bare wooden
floors show their scars again and ache for the forest.
He takes everything you have, this thief, but gives you one gift.

Each morning you open your eyes jealous as hunger, you walk
serpent-necked and dwarf-leggèd in the thief's distorting mirrors,
you go nakedly through the skyless moonless gardens and pagodas
of envy that he gives you, the thief's gift, your seeding wilderness.

Draco, the Dreaming Snake

Like a sigh in silence, the serpent,
oh, he dreams me, in his solar, in his naked house.

The serpent weeps if he thinks he is not wanted.
But he is. He dreams me. In his solar.
In his room for sun. In his pond of light.

Oh his great energy and his cleverness,
out of the naked house of the virgin he creeps,
skill and shame mixed in him,
and a vapour about his skin I shiver for,

glimpsing how it works, his magic,
but only a glimpse, he is all his own magician,
he sleeps as he travels over the clays and granites

of the land, never unemployed, always a worker,
yes, he gathers up the whirlwind of the sleepless
and finds some sleep for them. That is his work.
He dreams me. My serpent dreams me.

It is his intimidating but helpless gift.
In a fountain of pure undwindling water he dreams me,
he dreams me in the soft male heart of the lily,
its innocent roar.

He dreams me in my dream of the paper dead, the lost parents.
He dreams the shadow that does the washing-up
and the ironing in the new house. He dreams Mother Lion.

He dreams he is a serpent
who will be the last one of us all to die.
He dreams that all he wishes for will come true.
He dreams me.

In my hand I hold a golden coin covered with blood,
He dreams this.
He dreams this baby under the blue flower of my heart.

He dreams the fragmental stealth of my spirit.
He dreams my future, he dreams my past.
He dreams the breath of this bare room,
the chimney's old ache of blackened brick,
the ceiling a caul of faded paint,
the walls objecting to windows on principle,
doors opening and closing in an ardent future,
causing horror, fear, delight,
and all these dreams move in me like sex,
with little or no punishment or revenge.

Such is the serpent's business,
making something already beautiful even more possible,
the hiss of his hope touching a nerve.

Ancient serpenting tourist, he travels the world,
naked as celsius, naked as the great sophistication of glass,
naked as the flare of spice from your aroused skin,
naked as whatever again and again stretches its long coiled self
towards us, dreaming us and asking for our dreams.

We dream him a new skin to cocoon his aspen heart,
to clothe his whip of a spine; a perfect fit;
tender as an eyelid;
his new scales glitter like rain on his hooded head,
and he dreams us, dreaming him.

Overnight

I am pinning wet laundry on the line an hour
before summer bedtime,
my shadow in the moonshed night holds up
warm dripping gathers, soapy scallop-edged hems,
a smocking of wrung-out blouses
shepherdessing me through my chosen task.
My rough fingers pin up his hugging shirts,
his ten long white arms fly out in spirals of spray,
the wet tails of my skirts twist to snares and nooses,
a daughter's near-adolescent fashions tremble and dance,
the bath towels pull like tarpaulins. I haul
them all up on the line, giving them to the moon
for drying.

I thought I was not meant to be loved,
but these wet clothes weigh me down with love,
its luscious clumsiness, its terror and wit.
I look up at the moon.
He will do his share of the work, I know,
even though he's only at half-strength;
all night he will dry the clothes with his clean clannish breath.
They will not be called strangers by him.
I leave him bending forward over the garments like a lover
and come to you.

We are beyond clothes;
naked, our bodies pillowed and spelling out breath,
we are the long kite-ribboning lovers;

67

my flame of orgasm is innocence returning, yours breaks
on me like a sky of connubial indoor rain.

Out in the yard, the washing sways and lulls;
solemn as children, the pale plump dresses,
the collars and cuffs with their couvades of lace,
the fledgling buttons flouncing in moonlight,
a row of fluttering sentries not needing their colours
until morning,
when I slouch sleepily out and unpeg them, creased
and armour-stiff, missing the moon, fearing bird-breath,
eggshell-bridge sky, the expectations of day;
in the house they lie like elderly rustics,
awaiting the phoenix of the iron to smooth them back to life.
Alive again, they desire and cover our family nakedness.

The Horse Who Loves Me

I

The horse who loves me is strong and unsaddled.
He desires to learn nothing.
He sleeps standing, like a tree.
He lifts dawn on his willing shoulders.

I ride the horse who loves me,
hands twined in his bashful mane,
knees gripping his nut-butter flanks.

The horse who loves me goes on tiptoe,
his hooves tap the fiery earth.
The long leisure of his muzzle pleases me.

His smell is salt and primroses, honeycomb
and furnace. Oh the sweat of his glittering tail!
How he prances studiously, the horse who loves me.

68

The horse who loves me has no hobby but patience.
He brings me the gift of his honesty.
His big heart beats with love.
Sometimes he openly seeks a wife. But he returns to me.

The horse who loves me is one of the poor of Paradise.
He enjoys Paradise as such a loving horse might,
quietly watching the seven wonders of the night.

2

Look at my horse!
His neatly-plaited snowy tail
hangs like a fine finger between his pearly buttocks.
His name can be Desire, or Brother.

He does not complain of my weight on his back
any more than darkness complains of its loneliness.

The horse who loves me
wields the prick of pain that caps the dart of love.
We gasp at its pang,
then race for the scaled wall of the sky.

The horse who loves me
takes me beyond the lengths grief goes to,
beyond the strides joy makes,
beyond the moon and his sister the future.

This heaven-kissing horse of mine
takes me with him to his aerial home.
Below us, roofs grey, fields fade, rivers shiver, pardoned.
I am never coming back.

from *Clayman, Leatherman and Glassman*

CLAYMAN

(3)
He puts the broken slabs of dry tough white clay
in an old tin bath and pees on it gently
to moisten it; the best way, the old way.
Then he leaves the clay to soak and soften.

Returning, he pinches the clay, testing its pliancy.
He puts his fingers to his mouth, tasting.
The sweet odd taste like wine and raw egg and mashed swede,
its smell of mould and rain and alcohol
tell him it's ready. He adds
a fistful of ground flint, to increase the whiteness,
a pinch of calcined animal bone, to add translucence
and blessing.

He lifts the clay in both hands
and thuds it down on the wooden benchtop,
knocking it into preliminary shape
by hammering it repeatedly with his fists,
then pressing the weight of his spread hands
down on it; the air must be forced out.
He grabs the clay up, throws it down,
beats it with his fists again. He punches
and pummels it, groaning and urging himself on;
it must be done;
this is not the gentle time.

With a wire he splices the clay in two, like cheese;
examines it for air bubbles.
Walloping the two halves together with a clap of laughter,
he wedges the clay, pushing the softest clay out
in convexing folds further than the firmest seams of clay.
After much adroit pushing and pulling with his hands,

much gripping and slapping, thwacking and thumping,
thrashing and pounding, the boneless clay is ready.

(4)
He holds the first slab of her,
preparing to create his love from clay,
(from the female genre of mud, earth,
clay, white silt).

He looks for the first hint of her
within the mass that he belabours,
as he moulds, as he finger-carves,
as he pulls off the many veils of clay that enwrap her;
in his hands the clay is shuddering;
loiteringly, he coils, kneads, shapes, coaxes.

Sweating, he plumps the mound of white clay
to a rough torso shape; a woman;
he hugs the clay to his own breast
as he works, shaping base of throat,
rib-cage, collar-bone, breasts, waist
and slight flare of hips; the white torso
presses hard against his flat hand;
they are breast to breast.
Under his hands he feels clay, gristle, sinew.
He sets her on the table.
With fresh clay, he rolls the cylinder that will be her arms.

(5)
He holds a damp white boulder of clay in his hands.
It is bigger than a woman's head,
for the clay will shrink as it dries.
He places the lump of clay gently on the wooden board.
It is white and lopsided, vague, blind.
He sits a little way off, waiting to recognize her;
waiting for the clay to give him permission

to look for the woman it wants to be.
He is scared; his skills, his conviction,
his husbandry fade. His dream of making a woman
out of clay, her voice instructing him fade.

The palms of his hands flutter with energy that eludes his grip;
he dare not turn to look at the finished torso under her cloak
of sacking, nor at the perfect arms and legs lying
under similar blankets; waiting.

Why am I making this woman?
I have made her a beautiful room,
with polished floor, mirrors, flowers,
with silent curtains, a bed of fluffy satin,
raisins and chicory to eat.
Why am I making her?

Not for a sister, not for a mother.
A companion? A friend?

Like an islander alone, he needs her.
She alone can explain why he needs her.

CONCLUSION: WIVES AND WORKERS

These are the three workers, with their materials,
clay, leather, glass;
here are their wives, Lady Glass, Lady Black-Leather, and Lady
    Clay.

The men work in daylight,
they have the hands of their fathers,
the eyes and hearts of their mothers.

Clayman labours with the soft solid burden of clay.
He loves it like the ground under his feet, with ordinary
useful love. He develops his husbandry,
his hands unfaltering in the daylong odour of earth.

72

Above his head, the roof shines with gold
from ridge to eaves, the gilded house of the married man.

Leatherman unreels a long length of indolent tanned skin,
jetsam delicate as air. He strokes its spiced weave
like pulled-out lace from a lavish corsetry.
His blood-roots quicken and quiver like a beaten drum of feathers.
He works fast with template and broad knife; giving
leather its after-life.
It is his gift, flagrant, simple and secret.

Glassman breathes in a wisp of carbons.
Torment of glass dust hides in the mist of his lungs.
His lips murmur; incantation and joke,
incandescent forfeit.
He makes a crescent moon of wild robust glass,
letting the glass flow and shift, adaptable,
the vernacular of glass rustling.

The wives watch.

One came from the willing earth,
to live in his helpless boudoir,
under his bright sloping roof;
so that he will never be homesick.

One came from her man's love of leather;
her love is thin as sky, tough as whipcord.
His heart hangs from her wide and studded leather belt.

One came from his glass-wet dream,
his potent sigh;
her love is his one strong plank
from a wrecked ship of glass.
Over hurdles of glass, she leaps towards him.

One loves Glass and marries him.
One loves leather and marries Leather.
One loves earth and marries Clay.
There are long silent busy nuptials
in the nights;
each woman burns her own tongue in the flame of love.

Each Eva permits an Adam to create her;
so she may begin her work,
which is to finish his work for him.

Claywoman dissolves the pots and bowls in rain,
bringing them down to earth again.

Leatherwoman lets the killed leather graze,
solid from horn to hoof. The herds
look up, surprised, then feed again, big tongues
simplifying grass.

Glasswoman sets glass singing; the birds flock
and fuss; next, fruit ripens into colour, fragrance,
eloquent seed; real fish grunt through real water;
a world of glass goes free, learns life,
the weight of death.

Angel

The angel is coming down,
white-hot, feet-first,
abseiling down the sky.

Wingspan? At least the width
of two young men lying head to head,
James and Gary, their bare feet
modestly defiant, pointing north,
south.

The angel has ten thousand smiles,
he is coming down
smooth as a sucking of thumbs,

he is coming down on a dangle of breath,
in blazing bloodsilk robes.
See the size and dignity of his great toes!

He comes down in a steam of feathers,
a dander of plumes,
healthy as a spa,
air crackling round him.

Yes, he comes down
douce and sure-winged,
shouting sweetly through the smoke,
'J'arrive!'

Hovering on fiery foppish wings,
he gazes down at me
with crane-neck delicacy.

I turn my head from his furnace,
his drastic beauty . . .
he is overcoming me.

On my crouched back his breath's
a solid scorching fleece.
In my hidden eyes, the peep of him hurts.

He waits,
he will not wait long.

Flames flicker along my sleeve
of reverence as I thrust my hand
into the kiln of the seraph.

Howling, I shoulder my pain,
and tug out one feather,
tall as my daughter.

When I look up,
he's gone on headlong wings,
in a billow of smoulders,
sparks wheeling, molten heels

slouching the side wind. 'Adieu!'

Goodbye, I wave,
my arm spangled with blisters
that heal as I stare at the empty sky.

And the feather?
                    Is made of gold.
Vane and rachis, calamus
and down. For gold like an angel
joyeth in the fire.

'No pudieron seguir soñando'

'They could not go on dreaming.'

Storyteller North and Bystander South
stopped dreaming. So did East and West.

There was no more dreaming for Sun,
no more dreaming for Moon.

'No pudieron seguir soñando.'

No, they could not go on dreaming
For all the Horses, no dreams.

For all the Mirrors, no dreams.
No dreams for the Forest,
despite his noble descent.

There is no tomorrow.
They could not go on dreaming it.

There's no tomorrow for the Mountain.
No tomorrow for the Ocean.

No dreams for the sober Whale.
No dreams for Mouse or Wolf.
No dreams for anyone.

Even the Street Women,
women of the poorer sort; they stopped dreaming.

No tomorrow for the Child
with his taste for solitude.

'No pudieron seguir soñando.'

Downhill Night and Tell-tale Dawn
stopped dreaming. So did Ghosts and Wheels.

No dreams for Globe-trotter Horizon,
no dreams for that drifter, Air.
No dreams for the Flower of Venus.

Lion stopped dreaming. Money
stopped dreaming.

All the Masks stopped dreaming.
Not one Razor or Scarecrow,
Web or Bone dreamed.

There is no tomorrow.
They could not go on dreaming it.
No.

The thinnest pane of Glass,
the most nimble and leaping Door,
the most devout Dog. No,
they could not.

Women stopped dreaming. So did Men.
'No pudieron seguir soñando.'
How could there be a tomorrow,

when none of the Trees dreamed?

When there was no dreaming for Snow,
for clannish Ant or veil-winged
Bee? Ask them to dream.

They cannot.

For even the dirty Water in the Gutter
has stopped dreaming. And not one of any
three Foxes can dream. No Thumb can dream
nor any of the Fingers of any Hand.

78

For there are no more tomorrows.

For the Ship cannot dream
and turns to cloud. For Cloud cannot dream
and rolls away like a stone
but it is no Stone.

The Invisible Man cannot dream.
The Seen Woman cannot dream.
Even for them, no tomorrow.

'No pudieron seguir soñando.'
They could not go on dreaming.

For the River, there's no tomorrow.
No tomorrow for the Dove,
faithful in marriage, chaste in widowhood.

Silver stops dreaming. Iron stops dreaming.
Pearls cannot dream. Nor can
Ice, Jade, Rice, Dew. No Heart
is dreaming. No Tongue is dreaming.

There is no tomorrow.
They could not go on dreaming it.

No one could.
Not even the Rain could.
Not even the Sky.

Whenever an earthquake occurs,
our planet rings like a bell;
but it has stopped dreaming.

Not one Stone in the World is dreaming.
The last word of all
is in your mouth;
slide it between my lips;
let me taste the last of salt.

Looking for Love

This woman looking for love
has to mend all the sails
that a winter of storms has ripped
to shreds, she will be sewing for years.

This guy must be looking for love.
See how he crouches like a runner
before the race.

Another man looking for love
crawls smiling up the phosphor mountains
of hell, the burning acrid slopes.

Two teenage girls speeding along
the towpath on golden-wheeled bikes,
are they looking for love?
Or are their shadows flying
over the naked Thames enough for them?

This woman looking for love
finds one tear in the rain.
If love were the remains
of a small wild horse,
or the skull of a young boy
lost in the wreck
of 'The Association',
she would have found love.

Two spitting cats
couple in the moonlit yard.
Is this love? thinks the peeping child.
She hopes not.

This woman looking for love
gets the door slammed in her face.
He's got too many wives already . . .

This fella looks for love
in the National Gallery,
he thinks he's Little Christ
snuggling and glittering on a Renaissance lap;
mother's boy,

whereas his wife,
rehearsing the Virtues and their Contraries,
finds love without looking,
in a room on the fourth floor of an ethereal hotel;
she doesn't ask his name.

Big Cat

A windowful of cloud.
Rain on the big sloping glass roof
falls from a once-only sky.

The lovers shiver,
their tongues spate
in their mouths
with a why and a how;
they say now, now.

The room holds them in its history,
between its pages,
as they tap at heaven.

They shake in their silver lining.

The window holds its breath.

Then the lovers come.
Then sleep purrs in their throats
like a big cat guessing names.

Trick Horse

The trick horse is a bareback horse,
a holy horse
composed of many bare backs,
many couples in union,
near-naked men and women artfully entwined,
arranged in their copulations, loins
studded together so that their balancing bodies
create the body of a horse,

a yoga of sexy reciprocations.

The reason the trick horse brings good luck?
He's made from our inclination to fuck.

Men and women grip wrists, shoulder thighs,
weave, twine, dovetail, cling, clasp
and loll; are joined in the volupté
of their disguise. All support all.

It is an act of love, however they pose.
One woman's long swoop of dark hair—horsetail.

Yet the faces of these horse-makers
are as serious as any worshippers
in more austere religions; calm copulators,
the black-moustached men gazing about in sexual
reverie; the women, in gemmed bibs,
with pearl-studded noses, are just as grave

in their abandon. Though jewels of sweat
shiver on their golden skins, they assemble
as silently and devoutly as if in church
to make this estimable shameless mount.

One woman stretching her upper body forward
to make the horse's head,

(her glossed and outspread hair the mane),
grins and raises two hennaed index-fingers
to prick up the ears
of the animal of desire and delight.

Now comes the flower-garlanded rider
of this holy horse,
a girl thumb-belled, chime-toed,
a girl naked but for flowers and bells
and gold-braided bodice,
dancing towards her mount.

Now she lowers her baton of jasmine
and bows in greeting, the many eyes
of the horse watching her,
its many musks rising and clouding about her.

One man extends his linked hands,
making a stirrup for her gilded foot,
up she vaults,
with a leaping of bells,
scaling the carnal creature,
ascending her shivery gasping horse;
she squats and kisses the topmost balancing man,
who is persevering in his desire,
sinks herself down
upon her husband-saddle,
upon the pommel
of his stiff and risen phallus,
knees gripping,
flexing her haunches
till he's deep within her yoni;
and there she sits, radiant jockey,
astride, communing
with all the members of her love horse,
who quake in complicity and delight,
then steady, willingly taking her weight.

Now the girl rider, high upon her tantrick horse,
taps its composite flanks once
with her flowery rod;
this is the trick horse that all may ride,
that all may make.

She and her companions clip clop away in rapture.

Neighbour

Holding the rain in your arms
you grow wiser, wetter!
The sky is not too big for you,
you could carry that too,
like a tree-bride or a hill-wife.
My house opens its eyes
and lets you give it tears;
how it weeps! and finds itself
next to the flooded garden.

You bring me this rain
that turns you to one
who knows the rain by heart,
whose sleeves turn to rain,
whose hands hold the rain
but as if by accident,
whose memory is now only rain,
whose future is rain,
who brings me the passions
and security of the rain.

You play the rain like a musical instrument.
Is it horn or string or percussion?
It is all. It plays, you play it,
music spills and drums, strums and hums.

As you play you observe me
with the eyes of rain,
my poorest neighbour,
my strangest friend.
You sing to me in rain,
you joke in rain,
you put rain into my arms
like flowers young as the hills.
How I hope the rain never stops,
for every inch of rain
surely is gifted
and deserves to be loved
as well as you love it.

Georgette

No matter how often she moves the furniture
she can't find her Childhood.
It is named, after the fashion of hurricanes,
Childhood Georgette.
But where is it?
No matter how often she coaxes old chairs
into new places, she can't find her Childhood.
Father grumbles quietly up and down the steps.
Mussed and sweaty,
she pushes everything back against the walls.
She looks and looks. Childhood?
Big hands clap the sky, Father is sending the rain.
She pushes her little foster bike through the rooms,
searching.
Father is at the window with his stormy thoughts.
He is shaking his branches.
Too old for a kiss? laughs Father out in the rain.
Again and again
he and the rain know what's right and what's wrong.
She leans the tear-stained bike against the wall.

Childhood?
A nudge of thunder. Don't tell lies!
She puts the furniture back how it was, everything
stares back obediently at her. Father
is muttering one of his old songs
and peeping round the door. Rain calls
out the name she never liked.
The windows don't lift a finger. Now Father
in those mirrors
is smiling at his little poupée.
Now she rides on Father's shoulders,
seeing everything, interpreting nothing.
Georgette is riding. Ice and rain on the stairs,
all the rooms galloping round and round
and hurting, Father knows where her Childhood is.

Zoo Morning

Elephants prepare to look solemn and move slowly
though all night they drank and danced, partied
and gambled, didn't act their age.

Night-scholar monkeys take off their glasses,
pack away their tomes and theses,
sighing as they get ready for yet another long day
of gibbering and gesticulating, shocking
and scandalizing the punters.

Bears stop shouting their political slogans
and adopt their cute-but-not-really teddies' stance
in the concrete bear-pit.

Big cats hide their flower-presses, embroidery-frames
and watercolours;
grumbling, they try a few practise roars.
Their job is to rend the air, to devour carcasses,
to sleep-lounge at their vicious carnivorous ease.

What a life.
But none of them would give up show-business.

The snakes who are always changing,
skin after skin,
open their aged eyes and hinged jaws in welcome.

Between paddock and enclosure
we drag our unfurred young.
Our speech is over-complex, deceitful.
Our day out is not all it should be.
The kids howl, baffled.

All the animals are very good at being animals.
As usual, we are not up to being us.
Our human smells prison us.

In the insect house
the red-kneed spider dances on her eight light fantastics;
on her shelf of silence she waltzes and twirls;
joy in her hairy joints, her ruby-red eyes.

Delicious Babies

Because of spring there are babies everywhere,
sweet or sulky, irascible or full of the milk of human kindness.
Yum, yum! Delicious babies!
Babies with the soft skins of babies, cheeks
of such tit-bit pinkness, tickle-able babies, tasty babies,
mouth-watering babies.

The pads of their hands! The rounds
of their knees! Their good smells of bathtime
and new clothes and gobbled rusks!
Even their discarded nappies are worthy of them, reveal their powers.
Legions and hosts of babies! Babies bold as lions, sighing babies,
tricksy babies, omniscient babies, babies using a plain language

of reasonable demands and courteous acceptance.
Others have the habit of loud contradiction,
can empty a railway carriage (though their displeasing howls
cheer up childless women).
Look at this baby, sitting bolt upright in his buggy!
Consider his lofty unsmiling acknowledgement of our adulation,

look at the elfin golfer's hat flattering his fluffy hair!
Look next at this very smallest of babies
tightly wrapped in a foppery of blankets.
In his high promenading pram he sleeps sumptuously,
only a nose, his father's, a white bonnet and a wink
of eyelid showing.

All babies are manic-serene, all babies are mine,
all babies are edible, the boys taste best.
I feed on them, nectareous are my babies,
manna, confiture, my sweet groceries.

I smack my lips,
deep in my belly the egg ripens,
makes the windows shake,
another ovum-quake
moves earth, sky and me . . .

Bring me more babies! Let me have them for breakfast,
lunch and tea! Let me feast, let my honey-banquet of babies
go on forever, fresh deliveries night and day!

Faire Toad

'Foul toade hath a faire stone
in his head',
especially is this fine
in the heads of old and great toads;
the fairer the stone,
the stronger his venom.

88

Until today I never knew
toads shed their skins; in muck and mud,
agony and triumph of transformation,
the magic of the amphibian.

Faire toad feeds only on living prey.
He carries his heart in his throat.
But for the mating time
he lives the life of a recluse.

He climbs higher and spawns deeper
than cousin frog.
When man and wife toad embrace,
they do not cease for hours
their amorous encounter.

A toad may choose to live in water or earth.
Great is his capacity for fasting.

No, he does not spit fire.
No, he does not love women,
though in stories he is royal
as any frog.
He does not suck milk from cows.

Scholar-toad sees more than we see,
his eyes are eight times
more sensitive to light
than our human clarity.
Such glooms his eyes can pierce . . .

My lady toad gives herself
in wax, iron, silk and wood
on the wayside altars of Central Europe.

Luck shuffles
in to the parlour which a toad visits.

If you wish for his treasure,
do not torment him or dress him
in new silk;
but give him warmth, kindness,
pleasure; then he'll be buffoon
and priest, hopping
and processing in his khaki, bronze
and sepia swarth . . . leave
you his jewel-head in his will,
a faire and blood-hot ruby.

Taxing the Rain

When I wake the rain's falling
and I think, as always, it's for the best,

I remember how much I love rain,
the weakest and strongest of us all;

as I listen to its yesses and no's,
I think how many men and women

would, if they could,
against all sense and nature,

tax the rain for its privileges;

make it pay for soaking our earth
and splashing all over our leaves;

pay for muddying our grass
and amusing itself with our roots.

Let rain be taxed, they say,
for riding on our rivers
and drenching our sleeves;

for loitering in our lakes
and reservoirs. Make rain pay its way.

Make it pay for lying full length
in the long straight sedate green waters

of our city canals,
and for working its way through processes

of dreamy complexity
until this too-long untaxed rain comes indoors

and touches our lips,
bringing assuagement—for rain comes

to slake all our thirsts, spurting
brusque and thrilling in hot needles,

showering on to anyone naked;
or balming our skins in the shape of scented baths.

Yes, there are many who'd like to tax the rain;
even now they whisper, it can be done, it must be done.

Yule

On the tall green tree we have hung
the little golden masks of Bacchus,
the many little grins glinting and sparkling,
'oscilla ex alta suspendent mollia pinu,'
waving amulets from the tall pine,
as did the roman soldiers, revering
'the cedar in its bravery',
the sacred, ever-green, ever-living pole,
recalling in winter dark that other deathless tree
whose roots are deep in little-hell,
whose highest boughs uphold great heaven.
Sweet resins fill the house,
atop the tree stands Frau Sonne, shining one . . .
And here on the table is our Christmas cake,
'geologically sound, with one stratum of icing,
and one of marzipan, the whole superimposed
on alluvial darkness', and 'the vast globe
of plum-pudding, the true image of the earth,
flattened at the poles', from which the flame leaps,
as it leaps along the log of yule
by whose light we watch the year's wheel turn.
Now from the popped and plundered
red and golden paper crackers, we eagerly unfold
and don our Saturnalian hats of crepe
and beneath the luminous Kissing Bough
of mistletoe and woven green bay,
we kiss in a pre-Copernican way;
the sun moves, not us, not our earth!
We beg her to live again, arise from her winter death!
All the multitude of Bacchus' golden lips
move in smiling silent supplication.

Here is your tree, here are your children, Reine Soleil,
give us your gifts . . .

Flood

Water asleep
all across China,

cool days and nights
of water sleeping

and growling
in its sleep,

young dog water,

and stars wanting
to be held tight,

and the rain lingual
as ever,

and China folding hands
idiomatically,

and water expatiating
and dreamy,

and not writing anything down,
and the rivers

in endless revolution,
winding in psycho-sensual economy

round and round
the scenic perfumeries,

the hills and other illuminants:

water asleep
as it circles China,

inundating the palaces,
unplanning the cities,

and floating the Buddhas
downstream in their sleep.

Tigers

My girl shivers beside me
under the quilt she sewed us all last summer.

Perhaps she dreams Freud loses all his money
in a telepathy scam

or that she attends the first performance
of Mozart's *Faust*.

She dreams she is the Tsar's favourite child,
perhaps.

Perhaps in her dream a dowry-storm of Fabergé eggs
bounces off our roof,
glittery mad jewelled hail.

I love her.
She is more like god than anyone I know.
She dreams for so long!

I never expected to paint the world
as a holy world. But I do, now.

The higher you climb, she told me,
the better the view. Don't look down.

Weeping, she dreams of women blown
to ashes, flying away,

beyond towns, bridges—they cannot get
too far away . . .

. . . even from her . . .

Dream? Of course I dream.
But not like her. No, never like her.

I do not see the tigers.
I just hear them roar. And I shiver.

Outgrown

for Zoe

It is both sad and a relief to fold so carefully
her outgrown clothes and line up the little worn shoes
of childhood, so prudent, scuffed and particular.
It is both happy and horrible to send them galloping
back tappity-tap along the misty chill path into the past.

It is both a freedom and a prison, to be outgrown
by her as she towers over me as thin as a sequin
in her doc martens and her pretty skirt,
because just as I work out how to be a mother
she stops being a child.

Forgive

It is easy to forgive a lot of trees
for growing all together
and just call them a forest.

A round map of the world glitters
when you forgive it,
and rivers get wetter.

It is easy to forgive children,
you can think about them, far away,
in some nice apartment in New York, say,
or Macao,

running from one big sunny room to another,
and forgive them all the time,
they are like new shoes that hurt
without meaning to . . .

But it is hard to forgive someone
who used to be brave
and happy and as real
as the planet we all live on

when that person
smashes up everything you own
with small cold mean hands,
and then wants kisses . . .

And if that person doesn't even
want to be forgiven,
is he or she worth a week
of not being able to dream straight?

Tell me what you think.
Shall the women fly, or become trees
with dark green leaves that never fall?
Is it easy to forgive trees?

When you look at trees and people
do you want to forgive them
or paint them?
Or is it all much too sad—

so that for days it doesn't matter
if you are a man or a woman,
sighted,
or blind with a golden dog for eyes?

And hoping
is like finding out what happened in the past—
not possible.

The world has so many people in it!
But it forgives them all, not hoping
for anything.

It forgives even the important ones.
They are forgiven. Just like the trees.
Call them a forest. Let rain fall on them.

Waterlily Tradition

The women are singing in the patisserie,
their faces pencilled
by doubts, diets and genre friendships,

but he composes better songs
skinnydipping beautifully in my lily pond,
lolling against the Lucida and the Perry's Pink.

I wonder what else he will do to make me
feel so strange—there are so many possibilities.

While he floats and composes like a foundling
among copulant dragonflies and sleepy slithering terrapins,
I worry that nothing will last, nothing!

But then, remembering other lives I never speak about,
I feel more cheerful, and drift out
to my trustful garden where at the waterside
young Rossini is slicking back

his damp dago curls. How honestly he consumes
my candied patronage! He takes my hand,
glad to be haunted by me, and tells me,

'Childhood is often close to the waterlily
tradition, Madame—ruthless floating innocence,
too beautiful, too observed . . .'

What he says must be true, I know this,
just as I know one day he will betray me.
But for today I am content to be in tune with young Rossini

who says he can smell water a mile off
like a horse, and who composes best with rain on his lips.
He kisses me . . .

Now do you believe me when I say I love to sing?
It is my waterlily tradition.

Worse Things than Divorce

I was helping Dancey lift his wife April by her ears into the sky
(he was round today like someone a fish might imagine)
when a gang of blue-jeaned mothers, each with a tiny snuffling baby
floppily-strapped to her bosom, rushed us and rescued her.
That evening I surprised Dancey buttoning himself into one of her
   gowns.

Swathed in the soft bondage of her perilously-frail undergarments,
he said with a regal glare, 'Obviously I seek to detain her spirit,
Carol. But her perfumes are fading, minute by minute!'
He avoided red the least of all the colours in her wardrobe.
'Oh why did they take her from me!' he wept, his moustache
dribbling with tears. 'Now I am just like everyone else.' (Despairingly
he pulled one of her stockings down over his face.)

We parted friends, sometime in late summer, early autumn.
It rained and rained as he legged it past the Lloyd's Building,
lovely bright rain, you know?
so that everything had this golden-wet alchemique glitter,
especially the sky rainbowing high over the city of fierce mothers
and tiny babies and disappeared wives, the sky
where Dancey longed to reign with April.
'Darling,' he shouted, scampering along. 'April, darling!'
As he splashed away, he grew taller and taller,
like somebody a spider or a baby might imagine. 'Darling!'
His yells grew fainter, his head nudged the clouds . . .
And me? Here I am, ironing shirts, yawning, grumbling,
grinning at the whiff of sex that sneaks into the room,
just as if Dancey were here, saying, 'Lo, it is I . . . Everything is ok.'

Kingdom of Tiny Shoes

We are all dead, Lucy, Cush, Kilroy and me,
but we have about five or six ghosts each.
Imagine our embarrassment, here in the next world
where everything blazes with a terrible glassy
casino glamour, where it's never dark;
because for us the great egg of time is broken.

Because we all have so many ghosts,
there's a lot of singing,
dancing, gambling, drinking, depressions,
fights, shitting and blaspheming;

one of my ghosts and one of Cush's
go in for honey-eating,
we love it, spooning, yumming, lip-licking greedily.

For a long time we all refused to accept it,
being here. Then suddenly Cush said—
Okay. Here we are. At least the drinks are free.

Even here there are winter fogs
and mists and pictures of Lenin and Jesus
on the walls. There are golf courses,
movies and divorces. More and more of us arrive.
Girls fall from the air, naked.
Old men burst up through the ground.
Proudly their shaven-head ghosts rush to meet them,
welcoming them, touring the wreckage with them.
Sometimes royal dead arrive in style, by boat.

One of my ghosts is always sad. Again K
puts his best-ghost's arms around this sad one of me
and says, 'There is no baby, you had no baby, sugar.'
'I am unwilling to believe you,' retorts this ghost,
'I am sure there is a baby,' and she goes on
looking for baby and baby's ghosts.
So far this ghost of me has found several packets
of disposable nappies and a pair of tiny knitted shoes
and this gives her hope . . .
The rest of my ghosts just look on, blinking and sniggering,
I'm afraid, and even Lucy taps her big fanged skull,
shrugging at such foolishness.

THREE POEMS FOR MY ARTIST
COUSIN, JAMES GUNNELL

Artist in Ink

The octopus, artist in ink,
impulsively draws eight pictures at once,
but none are portraits of dry land,
as the scuba-diving critic remarks . . .

There are so many ways of painting,
especially with eight arms . . .
Why, the octopus uses only one colour,
notes the shark, that devourer of art,
circling, never sleeping, gnawing
the leg of the diver-cum-critic . . .

But the octopus just inks in his seascapes,
juicily uninfluenced,
his ocean floor abstracts
endlessly octaving . . .

Bird-Painter

The famous bird-painter hobbles by,
getting richer every step.

His pet ostrich follows him everywhere,
walking on soft white dust.

The early-summer mountains
are so beautiful and gawky

but he ignores them,
he is not a painter of mountains,

he limps round his garden
as if in the salon of Mesmer,
his pet bird watching.

The bird-painter closes his eyes,
traces his descent

through the maternal line,
for was it not

one of his long-ago mothers
who told him—

if you must paint,
first take singing lessons
from the birds.

Picasso is Right

On my bedroom wall
Father paints a beautiful picture
of the famous river that runs beside our house.

The river is black and all the clouds,
fields, thin shimmering houses, stars,
moons and bridges are black, cool and noir.
Soon the entire wall is black.

His river-painting is so beautifully black,
so wild, so percussive,
it makes me weep, on each of my tears
is painted a tiny curled-up baby, seahorse-neat.

Father shrugs off my praise.
'Picasso is right,' says Father,
'black is the only colour.
You can fly through black!'

'But, Father, where shall we fly?'
Father smiles and looks wise.
'To one of the smaller Slavic countries,
of course,' he cries,

'where they too have chosen black
out of all the colours that are . . .
the colour that makes everyone weep . . .'

Building a City for Jamie

I am building Jamie a city with plenty palaces
but no churches, the chandeliers are very difficult.
I fix cajoling windows for Jamie,
and embroider incessant doors as best I can.
'More is needed than just love,' says Jamie.

'Build me a city,' says Jamie, 'so beautiful
I'll never want to escape from it.
Dearest one, build it for me.
Let the city rise overnight in its wonder and law.'

How Jamie's little bared teeth shine, how he hugs me!

'Build me a city it will be worth fifty winters
deciphering,' says Jamie, 'let there be fountains
to wash away the evils of man, let a great river coil
through the city for you know I pray to regain the lost favour
of water . . .

I want my city to happen fast!
I want to be sitting in one of my cafés now,
eating dainties on the sly . . .
If you are my friend,' says Jamie, 'build me a city.
Build, beloved. Build!'

TWO

I lean over the plans of the city,
explaining everything to Jamie.
'Your city will have wish-bone weather,
the happiest backstreets anywhere in the world,
with houses painted in such anticipatory colours,
freshly-caught fish, lily, young-green, high-flying blue!
Here the moon will be no stranger,

104

a heart-shaped wall will surround Jamie's city . . .
Look at all this scaffolding,
the cold cages of steel, jambs and stanchions,
the webs and ichors of architecture,
dog-shat-on-sand-heaps, stacks of bricks,
sketched-out foyers, half-homes, spires sighing
and moaning to be in their rightful places . . .
See it all roll towards the radiance of the built, Jamie!'

'Oh!' says Jamie,
opening his eyes very wide.

THREE

With my bare hands I build a city for Jamie.
It is easier than I suspected. The city flies into my hands.

Swiftly I am raising towers for appreciating the moon
in Jamie's city, and many pavilions for obtaining tranquillity.
Quickly I am building a palace for the fishes' pleasure,
where in wide deep tanks his emerald utopics
pace and dream.

Gently I am making a nine-span bridge over Jamie's river,
delicate as any living creature.
The sky that sees itself in the river's clearness
is the sky of another world, you can tell at once.

Tearfully I am building a tomb for Jamie's three favourite wives,
making sure there is a false door in the tomb wall
for the deceased ladies to come and go as they please.

And everywhere in the city I plant trees in alphabetical order.
At once they begin blossoming; almond, cherry, may and plum.

Also I make sure old things are in the city,
rusty bedsteads, cracked cups and plates, some cupboards
stuffed with old maps, balls of saved string,
stained recipe books, worn shoes, faded sheet music of rueful songs.

I say, 'There must be many sorts of things in your city,
Jamie, even the ugly and old.'
At this he bends his knees, squat-howling, 'No gods! No gods!'
and beating the air with his hands, until I bring him a cool drink.

FOUR

From one of the many tremendous roofgardens in Jamie's city
we look down at the open-air library
under its giant umbrella of blue slate. 'Any one
of those books,' says Jamie, pointing, 'might become a woman.
Between the covers, like a room of gold and crimson holidays,
sultry pages shuffle her story of white under-things.
There's the rustle of a jacket,
with quick fingers she amuses herself undoing
the black hooks and eyes of print—and not minding
her lack of brothers and sisters,
she smoothes her hands down over her naked flanks,
approving the strength of her pelvis, that narrative!
(She has arrived with no luggage, you see.)
Or will you shape her, my charmer, from my rib as I sleep?'

FIVE

In the Arbour of He Who Flees The Anger
Of His Brother, Jamie is crying.

In The Garden Of The Promise Of Rain
Jamie thinks he's burying his brother's heart.

Across The Courtyard Of The Tiny Shoes,
Jamie comes to me with quick vexed steps.
'Where is my city?' he sobs, forgetting everything.

'Where is my city
that is a copy and a shadow of heaven,
my city that smells of woman's semen,
Jamie's city?'

SIX

'This is your city, Jamie.
Here it is.'

O Jamie, you are getting sleepy and not listening!
Snuggle down in my arms,
safe in this city that I built from memory.

Tomorrow when you wake in our room of interesting squalor,
asking: 'Was there really a city, a city for Jamie?'
I'll say lightly, 'No, you were just dreaming, baby. There is no city.'

'No city!' you'll frown, shivering,
as I shake my head and lie to you for your own good,
'No city?'

No city. Of course not.

OXFORD POETS

Fleur Adcock
Moniza Alvi
Joseph Brodsky
Basil Bunting
Tessa Rose Chester
Daniela Crăsnaru
Greg Delanty
Michael Donaghy
Keith Douglas
D. J. Enright
Roy Fisher
Ida Affleck Graves
Ivor Gurney
David Harsent
Gwen Harwood
Anthony Hecht
Zbigniew Herbert
Tobias Hill
Thomas Kinsella
Brad Leithauser
Derek Mahon
Jamie McKendrick

Sean O'Brien
Alice Oswald
Peter Porter
Craig Raine
Zsuzsa Rakovszky
Christopher Reid
Stephen Romer
Eva Salzman
Carole Satyamurti
Peter Scupham
Jo Shapcott
Penelope Shuttle
Goran Simić
Anne Stevenson
George Szirtes
Grete Tartler
Edward Thomas
Charles Tomlinson
Marina Tsvetaeva
Chris Wallace-Crabbe
Hugo Williams